The
KINGDOM
OF GOD HAS COME

APMI Publications
a division of Alan Pateman World Missions
P.O. Box 17,
55051 Barga (LU),
Tuscany, Italy

The KINGDOM
OF GOD HAS COME

Walking in the Footsteps of the First
Apostles: Jesus Christ, the Cornerstone

Martial LeBras NONO

BOOK TITLE:
The Kingdom of God Has Come
WRITTEN BY MARTIAL LEBRAS NONO
ISBN: 978-1-909132-17-7
eBook ISBN: 978-1-909132-18-4

Copyright 2025 Martial LeBras Nono

All rights reserved under International Copyright Law. Contents and/or cover may not be reproduced in whole or in part in any form without the express written consent of the Publisher.

Published By:
APMI Publications
In Partnership with Truth for the Journey Books
Email: publications@alanpatemanworldmissions.com
www.AlanPatemanWorldMissions.com

Acknowledgements:
Cover Design Copyright APMI
Senior Editor/Publisher: Dr. Alan Pateman
Editing/Proofreading/Research: Dr. Jennifer Pateman
Computer Administration/Office Manager: Dr. Dorothea Struhlik
Cover Image Credit: www.PosterMyWall.com

Dedication

To the **Almighty GOD,** the **Author of my life,**
To the **Lord JESUS CHRIST,** my **Saviour, Redeemer,** and **King,**
And to the **Precious HOLY SPIRIT,** my ever-present **Helper, Comforter,** and **Guide.**

HalleluYaH! Blessed be the name of the LORD, who has done, is doing, and will continue to do great, miraculous, and marvellous things in my life, that I may testify before His children and in the nations.

I dedicate this book in loving gratitude:

- To my parents, **NONO Ngansop Elisee** and **FOSSO Jeannette,** who taught me the fear of the Lord and showed me the way to Christ from an early age. Your unwavering prayers, godly counsel, and love have built a strong foundation for my walk with God.

- To my family — **my brothers, sisters, nephews, and nieces** — your presence, encouragement, and faith have been a gift of strength and joy.

- To the beloved brethren of **Go and Preach to All Nations Ministry** and **Grow With Christ,** who have stood with me in prayer, love, and faithful fellowship. This book is part of the fruit of our shared obedience and labor in Christ.

- And to the **Body of Christ worldwide** — especially those who seek, proclaim, and live the message and power of the Kingdom of God.

May this book be a trumpet to awaken hearts, renew minds, and prepare the way for the return of the King.

Truly, The Kingdom of God Has Come.

Table of Contents

	Acknowledgment	9
	Foreword	13
Chapter 1	The Primitive Church	17
Chapter 2	As Described By the Book of Acts	29
Chapter 3	Only Possible By Jesus & the Holy Spirit	45
Chapter 4	The Kingdom of God has Come	63
Chapter 5	The Prayer of Faith	75
Chapter 6	Christ in Science (Laminin Protein)	85
	Endnotes	97

Acknowledgment

All **glory, honour, and praise** be to the **Sovereign King,** the **LORD GOD Almighty** —Creator of the heavens and the earth, and **Author of this message.** By His Spirit, His grace, and His unfailing love, these words have been birthed and brought forth.

To **JESUS CHRIST,** the risen King, be all the glory, both now and forevermore.

As part of my acknowledgment, I wish to honour the Word of God, which has been the foundation of my faith and the guiding light of my life. Specifically, the Book of Acts of the Apostles has deeply stirred within me an unquenchable thirst for the things of God's Kingdom. It has illuminated my heart, igniting a fervent passion for Christ and driving me forward on my journey of faith. This book has opened my eyes to see the Church of God from a different perspective, a vision that longs to see the Church return to the original message of the Kingdom of God, as it was in the primitive Church, and as it should be at the coming of Christ. This book is the foundation of revival, with the first Apostles as the foundational pillars, empowered by the Holy Spirit of God.

With a heart full of gratitude, I express sincere thanks to:

- My beloved parents, **NONO Ngansop Elisee** and **FOSSO Jeannette**—thank you for your enduring prayers, godly example, and deep faith. You introduced me to Christ from an early age and laid a spiritual legacy that continues to guide and bless my walk with the Lord. You have truly been vessels of God's love and counsel.

- My cherished **brothers, sisters, nieces, and nephews** —your love, support, and presence have been a constant encouragement and a divine gift to my life.

- **Apostle Dr. Alan** and **Dr. Jennifer Pateman,** faithful servants of Christ whose lives shine with wisdom and a passion for building Kingdom leaders. Your encouragement, love, and unwavering commitment to the ministry have been pillars of strength. Thank you for your prayers and tireless dedication in the careful proofreading of this manuscript.

- **Elder Tagne Lucien,** a humble preacher and teacher of the Word, who has faithfully walked with me since the beginning of my journey in Christ. From

Acknowledgment

my conversion to this very moment, your prayers, encouragement, and Spirit-led teachings have drawn me closer to Jesus and laid spiritual foundations in my life.

- **Apostle Dr. Benjamin Ayim Asare,** whose faithful prayers and steadfast support have been a source of strength and inspiration for writing this book.

- **Dr. Dorothea Struhlik,** for her encouragement and support during my time at **LICU**.

- The beloved saints of **Go and Preach to All Nations Ministry** and **Grow With Christ** — your unwavering faith, encouragement, and relentless pursuit of God's Kingdom have been an anchor in this calling. Your intercession, partnership, and love continue to bear fruit for the Glory of Christ.

- **Prof. Zacharias Tanee Fomum,** a preacher, teacher, and disciple of Christ, whose writings continue to illuminate the path of radical discipleship. His uncompromising message of the Kingdom has stirred within me a relentless pursuit of God's purpose. His profound teachings and deep passion for the Kingdom of God have continually challenged and inspired me toward radical obedience and purpose in Christ.

- **Derek Prince,** a faithful Bible teacher, whose doctrinal clarity and anointed teaching have laid essential spiritual foundations in my walk with the Lord. His Spirit-anchored ministry laid foundational truths in my heart. His clarity in the Word and authority in the Spirit have been a lamp in my walk with Christ.

- **Evangelist Reinhard Bonnke,** through whom the Lord awakened in me the fire of evangelism. His bold preaching and deep love for souls ignited a holy burden that continues to burn within me by the Spirit of God.
- To every **servant of God**—pastors, missionaries, evangelists, intercessors, teachers, and ministry leaders—who has ever poured into my life through a word, a prayer, or an act of faithful love: I thank you. Heaven remembers.
- To all those who have supported the publication of this book, both prayerfully and financially, your generosity, faith, and investment in this project have made this work possible. Your contribution will bear eternal fruit as you have partnered with me in the work of the Kingdom. I thank you from the depths of my heart.

May this book sound as a trumpet to declare: The Kingdom of God Has Come! To the King be all the glory, now and forever. Amen.

Foreword

Apostle Martial Lebras Nono is an accomplished student of LICU. This book, which began as a study—a collection of research papers—reflects his earnest pursuit of understanding, rooted in Scripture, early Church history, and the living work of the Holy Spirit. Yet what you now hold in your hands is far more than an academic exploration. It is a call to rediscover the richness of a faith that is both intellectually grounded and spiritually transformative.

Beginning with the foundation of the primitive Church (our model) and the events recorded in the Book of Acts, Apostle Nono invites readers to trace the vibrant heartbeat of early Christianity. But the journey does not stop in the past—it draws a clear line to our present reality, revealing that what was possible then remains possible now, through Jesus Christ and the empowering presence of the Holy Spirit.

Each chapter builds with care, offering biblical insight, practical reflection, and moments of awe. From the primitive Church, through the Book of Acts, into the ministry of the Holy Spirit, and even the molecular mysteries of science, Apostle Nono shows us that the Kingdom of God is not a distant hope, but a present and living reality.

Particularly striking is the chapter on the Laminin protein, where Apostle Nono offers a compelling glimpse into how God's design is imprinted even at the cellular level—reminding us that faith and science are not at odds, but in harmony when rightly understood.

Whether exploring the Kingdom of God, the prayer of faith, or the scientific marvel of Laminin, the message is clear: God's design is not only historical—it is ongoing, intimate, and deeply personal.

This is a book that seeks to stir both mind and spirit. It challenges assumptions, affirms truth, and leaves the reader with a renewed sense of awe at the nearness and greatness of God.

So, whether you come with questions or conviction, whether as a lifelong believer or someone seeking deeper meaning, 'The Kingdom of God Has Come' will encourage, challenge, and inspire you to experience the power of a faith deeply rooted in both Word and Spirit.

Foreword

Far more than just another good read, this book is a tool for spiritual renewal—one that will stretch you, strengthen you, and draw you ever closer to the One who still moves, heals, and builds His Church today.

Apostle Alan Pateman, Ph.D.,
founder of Alan Pateman World Missions

Chapter 1

The Primitive Church

A Model to be Followed By The Church Today

Every man, tribe, society, organisation, country, or nation has a history and thus does the Church of God. In some cultures, like among the Africans, people give much value to their past and the traditions of their ancestors. Thus, in this kind of society, most people go forth in life while keeping an eye on the past to know and understand their present situation, especially when it comes to spirituality, religion, and tradition.

In secondary school, they used to teach us that history is the study of past events. In other words, past events need to be studied and understood to understand the available information to reconstruct the past. This implies that "history is the interpretation of the past in the light of data gathered."[1]

From a biblical view what has been in the past will be in the future, meaning that there is nothing happening today that doesn't have its roots somewhere in antiquity: "What has been is what will be, and what has been done is what will be done, and there is nothing new under the sun" (Ecclesiastes 1:9).

In the same way, as it is in every culture, society, and tribe, the Church of God also has a history. This starts from the series of events that were recorded in the Scriptures about the children of Israel, the coming of the Messiah and the Holy Spirit as predicted by the law and the prophets, and the birth of the early Church.

It is important to note that: "a place for history in Christian faith cannot be overemphasised."[2] This is thanks to the fact that the Christian faith originates from the history of a God who revealed Himself to humanity in the person of Jesus Christ.

Thus, the present true Church of God can only reflect the primitive Church that was built by God himself unto the foundation of the apostles and the prophets with Jesus as the cornerstone.

> *So, then you are no longer strangers and aliens, but you are fellow citizens with the saints and members of the household of God, built on the foundation of the apostles and prophets, Christ Jesus himself being the cornerstone,*

in whom the whole structure, being joined together, grows into a holy temple in the Lord.

(Ephesians 2:19-21)

Therefore, for the Church to be efficient in a biblical way and truly reveal the God creator, and founder of the Church, the disciples of today must be inspired, influenced, and shaped by the lives of our past heroes in faith, starting from the first century with the first apostles and the primitive Church throughout the centuries till today.

There is no Church Without the Holy Spirit

The Church was birthed in the Holy Spirit of God. Before His death on the cross, the Lord Jesus had started speaking about the birth of the Church and the coming of the Holy Spirit. The word Church was first mentioned in the Gospel of Matthew. "And I tell you, you are Peter, and on this rock, I will build my Church and the gates of hell shall not prevail against it" (Matthew 16:18).

Speaking of Jesus and the Holy Spirit, John the Baptist said: "I baptise you with water for repentance, but he who is coming after me is mightier than I, whose sandals I am not worthy to carry. He will baptise you with the Holy Spirit and fire" (Matthew 3:11).

In other words, there will be no outpouring of the Holy Spirit without Jesus being glorified and there will be no Church without the supernatural encounter of the first disciples with the Holy Spirit.

Before His death, just as John the Baptist announced the coming of Jesus, Christ Himself promised to His disciples the coming of the Holy Spirit. "Nevertheless, I tell you the truth: it is to your advantage that I go away, for if I do not go away, the Helper will not come to you. But if I go, I will send Him to you" (John 16:7). This suggests that there will be no Church without the coming of the Holy Spirit. His coming was a great advantage for the Church, for he is the Helper of the members of the Church.

What is the Church?

Generally, when people hear about the word Church what first comes to their mind is a building in a particular geographical location used for religious purposes such as worship, sermons, and prayers. Some people will refer to a denomination with a name e.g., the Pentecostal Church, the Protestant Church, the Roman Catholic Church, or the Evangelical Church.

Others see it as an organisation with the head being the founder or the leader of the organisation. The truth is that none of these concepts truly define the Church. There is only one Church and one head, Jesus Christ.

Looking at the Church just as a specific and separate building that is built for worship or Sunday services would have been foreign to believers of the primitive Church. This is because they didn't have such and didn't operate in this concept of Church being a specific building, rather they met in houses of members.

The Primitive Church

"Greet also the Church in their house. Greet my beloved Epaenetus, who was the first convert to Christ in Asia" (Romans 16:5). "The Churches of Asia send you greetings. Aquila and Prisca, together with the Church in their house, send you hearty greetings in the Lord" (1 Corinthians 16:19).

How can we then truly define the word Church? The English word "Church" comes from the Greek word "Ecclesia" which means *"the called-out ones."*

In the Greek language, this also refers to an elected parliament, a group of people "call out" to govern. In the New Testament, the word "ecclesia" refers to "the call out ones" of Jesus Christ. "Called out ones," from where? From the world. In the Old Testament the children of Israel were called out from Egypt – the type of the world.[3]

Therefore, the word Church will refer to believers rather than a building. That's why apostle Paul said to the Church in Corinth: "Do you not know that your body is a temple of the Holy Spirit within you, whom you have from God?" (1 Corinthians 6:19)

Sinners who are called out of the world to follow Jesus, worship, and serve God in the name of Jesus Christ through the Holy Spirit form the true Church of God. The building alone with members who didn't come out of the world through a true repentance will never be the Church of God.

When a building was mentioned in the New Testament, it was in relation to the people (the Church) that met there for fellowship or worship. It was much later, when

Christianity was legitimatised and had gained much affluence in Roman Empire, particularly, after the conversion of Emperor Constantine in the fourth century that the word Church came to mean the building where the people met.

Our contemporary time has further imported other meanings into the concept of Church; so that the word Church is now used to refer to particular denomination. The truth is that the word Church, as already stated actually means a group of believers.[4]

Who is the Holy Spirit?

The following paragraphs aim to answer the question of the identity of the Holy Spirit. Though there is a lot to say about the Holy Spirit, these outlines will give a brief description of the person of the Holy Spirit which is necessary to understand this work.

I believe that throughout the history of the Church the Holy Spirit has not been fully understood by believers. But why? Is it because He is hidden or far from the Church? No! but it is rather because the Church of today has evolved with the world forgetting that the Church is supposed to be a group of people called out of the world, even though they are in the world.

Many false theories and concepts have led to the definition of who the Holy Spirit is to most believers today. The Holy Spirit is therefore not who religion or religious people may say He is, He is who the Scripture says He is.

An immediate answer to the question defining the title of this section is that "the Holy Spirit is God in action on the earth", "He is the power of Pentecost."[5] "The Holy Spirit is the Third Person of the Trinity at work on earth."[6] That is, He is God the Spirit who was before and was from the beginning of everything.

Entering deep in the revelation of the Scripture, three distinct persons present themselves with each of them being God: God the Father, God the Son, and God the Holy Spirit. Among the three, the Holy Spirit is the first person that is mentioned individually in the Scriptures: "And the Spirit of God was hovering over the face of the waters" (Genesis 1:2).

Each person of the Godhead has a particular realm of action: "The Father dwells in the heavenly realm; Jesus is seated at the right hand of the Father, with the authority to govern the entire universe; and the Holy Spirit is active on the earth, leading the Church."[7] Thus, the Holy Spirit is the supernatural God Himself active in the Church with His supernatural power, gifts, and fruits for the Glory of Jesus Christ.

The Beginning of the Church
& The Outpouring of the Holy Spirit

Now that the foundations of the concept of "Church" and the person of the Holy Spirit have been laid down. Let's now talk about the birth of the Church. The coming of the Holy Spirit which marked the birth of the Church should not just be taken from the perspective of the New Testament. Long ago even before the coming of the Messiah on earth, the Holy Spirit was already promised by God the Father to the Children of Israel.

"And it shall come to pass afterward, that I will pour out my Spirit on all flesh; your sons and your daughters shall prophesy, your old men shall dream dreams, and your young men shall see visions. Even on the male and female servants in those days I will pour out my Spirit" (Joel 2:28-29).

Although there are different theological points of view on when this prophecy was or will be fulfilled, this work agrees with the belief that the first stage of this prophecy was accomplished at Pentecost, when apostle Peter cited these verses from the book of Joel in response to the inquiries of the multitude (Acts 2:17-21). On this day the Holy Spirit started the first Church also known as the primitive Church.

It was in 29 AD at the annual Jewish festival held 50 days after Christ's crucifixion, called the day of Pentecost. That morning, the Spirit of God burst upon the world in reality, not as a sweet influence but literally as a hurricane. He announced his own arrival with the miracle of one hundred and twenty disciples speaking in tongues. This noisy outburst attracted the first Christian congregation.[8]

Also, the outpouring of the Holy Spirit on the day of Pentecost as written by Luke in the book of Acts of Apostles chapter two describes the fulfilment of Jesus's promise to send the Holy Spirit. The promised Holy Spirit was coming to glorify Christ through the Church. "He will glorify Me, for He will take what is mine and declare it to you" (John 16:14).

The Primitive Church

The promised Holy Spirit came to empower disciples who came out of the world to worship and serve God. One condition for His coming was the unity of the believers, that's why Jesus said: "And behold, I am sending the promise of my Father upon you. But stay in the city until you are clothed with the power from on high" (Luke 24:49).

Therefore, the Church comes out of unity and not out of division, for the Holy Spirit through which the Church is birthed is one with the Son and the Father, i.e., God is in perfect unity with Himself and so is (or should be) the true Church.

The purpose of the empowerment was not for the glory of men or self-pride but for the Glory of God. Those who received the Holy Spirit were to become witnesses of Jesus Christ, and the birthed Church was to go from town to town, village to village, and all over the world to preach the Gospel of Jesus Christ. "But you will receive power when the Holy Spirit has come upon you, and you will be my witnesses in Jerusalem, and in all Judea and Samaria and to the end of the earth" (Acts 1:8). Therefore, the true Church is active in Evangelism as the Holy Spirit is active in the Church.

Hence there is no efficient Evangelism without the Holy Spirit, and no Church exists without Evangelism. This means that one cannot talk of the Church without the great commission and the Holy Spirit who leads and helps in the making of disciples. Let's see what happened on that day when the Church started. After, the Baptism of the disciples with the Holy Spirit, they were all filled with the Holy Spirit and Peter stood up to preach to the multitude present that day (Acts 2:14-41).

The Fruits of The Church

The first disciples in the primitive Church were living in perfect harmony and fellowship. Every true Church of Christ should produce and manifest what I call the fruits of the Church. These fruits are found in Acts 2:37-47. These believers devoted themselves to the teachings of the apostles; steadfast fellowship; the breaking of bread from house to house and the prayers, evangelism, and the baptism of the new converts, praise, and worship.

It is difficult to find in the Church today true love, fellowship, and pure apostolic biblical-based teaching. This is mostly because many attendees in the Church are visitors and not true members of the Church of God: "Visitors: These are names entered that are neither members nor adherents of the Church."[9] "We know that sometimes people come to the Church with different opinions and agendas, many Church folks have not fully committed to the Church. The local pastor must define those who are members and visitors."[10]

Also, many find themselves today in the Church without knowing the vision of the Church and without passing through repentance and conversion. "Many people were born in Christian homes and yet do not know really what the Church is all about. They claim to be a Christian, but their mind-set is quite opposite."[11] This was not the case in the primitive Church. The first apostles were focused on the preaching of the Gospel to make disciples rather than just making unbelieving believers. "Paradoxically we have Churches full of unbelieving believers?! What a pitiful oxymoron!"[12]

In Summary

It can be concluded that there will be no Church without the person of the Holy Spirit through which the Church was birthed. This Church is far more than being just a building or Christian denomination, but it is the people who are the Church i.e., the *"called-out ones."* The Church of God cannot be reduced to a specific building in a particular location as the bible teaches us that the first disciples met in homes of members.

Every true Church of God should have its foundation on the true apostolic teaching that was passed unto us by the first believers with Christ as the cornerstone. They were working with the Holy Spirit and were united. All were clothed with the power of the Holy Spirit to witness Jesus Christ as Lord and Saviour and not for their self-glory.

Because they were focused on the great commission and they aimed to glorify God, they could bear many fruits, which is the sign that they were true disciples of Christ and part of the true Church of God. "By this my Father is glorified, that you bear much fruit and so prove to be my disciples" (John 15:8).

Chapter 2

As Described By the Book of Acts

Luke's Sequel

The book of the Acts of the Apostles is presented as the second volume of a work on the beginnings of Christianity. This book was written by Luke, the physician; "Luke the beloved physician greets you" (Colossians 4:14), to Theophilus as an addition to his first book, the Gospel of Luke.

> *In the first book, O Theophilus, I have dealt with all that Jesus began to do and teach, until the day when he was taken up, after he had given commands through the Holy Spirit to the apostles whom he had chosen.*
>
> *(Acts 1:1-2)*

The Gospel of Luke relates "all that Jesus began to do and teach" (Acts 1:1). The book of Acts of the Apostles "serves as a bridge document that links the Gospels to the New Testament letters."[1] This book begins with the ascension of Jesus, and the birth of the Church, and narrates the story of how the Gospel was spread far beyond the vicinity of the Jewish community to the extremities of the World.

You will be My Witnesses to the Ends of the Earth

"But you will receive power when the Holy Spirit has come upon you, and you will be my witnesses in Jerusalem and in all Judea and Samaria, and to the end of the earth" (Acts 1:8).

In the first part of Acts of the Apostles (Chapters 1-12), Luke records several events that occurred during the time of the first disciples in the early Church. The author of the book 'Apostles: Can the Church Survive without Them?' emphasised how the Apostles of the Lamb "The original twelve (minus Judas),"[2] plus Matthias as the number twelve, received the Holy Spirit, preached the Gospel, and planted Churches throughout Israel while setting the foundation on how a Church needs to be organised and directed.

"And the wall of the city had twelve foundations, and on them were the twelve names of the twelve Apostles of the Lamb" (Revelation 21:14). "And they cast lots for them, and the lot fell on Matthias, and he was numbered with the eleven Apostles" (Acts 1:26).

In the second part of the book (Chapter 13-28), Apostle Paul, the first among what we call the ascension apostles, becomes not only the central figure of the early Church but also:

> *A "pivot" in that he was not only the last of the Apostles of the Lamb (who actually saw the risen Lord Jesus Christ) but was also the first of a new series of apostles, called the ascension apostles.*[3]

Also, Luke establishes two parallels concerning the life and organisation of the Church of Jerusalem (Acts 2:42-47; 4:32-35) giving a structure to the book's first chapters. Then, another parallel is set between Apostles Peter and Paul who "are the main protagonists"[4] in the history, the organisation, and the functioning of the early Church under the influence of the Holy Spirit, through which the Church was birthed.

"I will Build My Church"

The parallel is very useful for the Church today to avoid heresies in the setting, organisation, and functioning of the Church in that Jesus said to Peter: "And I tell you, you are Peter, and on this rock, I will build my Church, and the gates of hell shall not prevail against it" (Matthew 16:18). That is, on Peter and the other Apostles of the Lamb, the Lord Jesus Christ set the foundation on how His Church should function and be organised.

> *Consequently, you are no longer foreigners and strangers, but fellow citizens with God's people and also members of his household, built on the foundation of the apostles and prophets, with Christ Jesus Himself as the chief*

cornerstone. In Him the whole building is joined together and rises to become a holy temple in the Lord.
(Ephesians 2:19-21 NIV)

This model was then passed faithfully on to the ascension apostles, with Paul as the first among this group of apostles. Therefore, the key was passed from Jesus on to the Apostles of the Lamb, who in turn passed it over to the ascension apostles, who finally passed it over to the present Church. That's why Paul said:

According to the grace of God given to me, like a skilled master builder I laid a foundation, and someone else is building upon it. Let each one take care how he builds upon it. For no one can lay a foundation other than that which is laid, which is Jesus Christ.

Now if anyone builds on the foundation with gold, silver, precious stones, wood, hay, straw each one's work will become manifest, for the Day will disclose it, because it will be revealed by fire, and the fire will test what sort of work each one has done.
(1 Corinthians 3:10-13)

This means that no other foundation can be laid by an apostle or a prophet in the present Church if this does not take its origin from Jesus Himself as the cornerstone, and the first Apostles as those who laid the foundation of the Church, as mentioned in the book of Acts.

To avoid that another foundation is laid while building the Church today, a parallel between the book of Acts of the

Apostles and the present Church should be established, to serve as a model.

The Church of Jerusalem and its Organisation

Before the ascension, Jesus told His disciples not to depart from Jerusalem until they received the baptism of the Holy Spirit.

And while staying with them he ordered them not to depart from Jerusalem, but to wait for the promise of the Father, which, he said, "you heard from me; for John baptised with water, but you will be baptised with the Holy Spirit not many days from now."

(Acts 1:4-5)

Through the Holy Spirit, they received the power, insight, strength, capacity, and Leadership authority of Christ to start the early Church and organise it according to Christ, as the Holy Spirit was to teach and help them in everything. "But the Helper, the Holy Spirit, whom the Father will send in my name, he will teach you all things and bring to your remembrance all that I have said to you" (John 14:26).

After the resurrection of Jesus, the hope of the first disciples was restored. Everything started in Jerusalem and Judea, then spread to Samaria and to the end of the earth. They are to follow the model set and given by Jesus, for:

The apostles are thinking of the kingdom in terms of the promises made to Israel and the restoration of national sovereignty, but Jesus has in mind a larger vision of the Kingdom. Before it comes, the Church must proclaim the Gospel of Jesus Christ to all people everywhere in the power of the Holy Spirit.[5]

The Leadership of the Church in Jerusalem

In the area of leadership, again the early Church is our model. The Church has the mission of preaching the Gospel of the Kingdom all over the globe before Jesus returns to establish His Kingdom: "He said to them, 'It is not for you to know times or seasons that the Father has fixed by his own authority'" (Acts 1:7).

The Weapon of Prayer:

Jesus said: "The gates of hell shall not prevail against it (the Church)" (Matthew 16:18). Prayer is one of the spiritual weapons that God gave to His Church for spiritual warfare. Derek Prince who was an anointed teacher of the bible said in one of His books: "On the basis of much study and personal experience, I believe Scripture reveals four main spiritual weapons of attack. These are the following: prayer, praise, preaching, and testimony."[6]

So, it would be unfair to talk about the leadership of the Church without talking about what makes the success of leadership in the Church through the Holy Spirit, that is prayer. The first disciples started the Church in prayer: "All these with one accord were devoting themselves to prayer, together with the women and Mary the mother of Jesus, and his brothers" (Acts 1:14).

"And when they had prayed, the place in which they were gathered together was shaken, and they were all filled with the Holy Spirit and continued to speak the Word of God with boldness" (Acts 4:31).

Continuous Spiritual Warfare

Knowing that the Church of God is engaged in continuous spiritual warfare, a true, organised, and successful leadership with a Christ-centred functioning can only exist if there is prayer. In the book, "Discover your Ministry in Local Church," the writer states: "Prayer is a weapon in the hand of the believer. Every leader is responsible to see to it that his/her own personal life is strong and that the congregation practice prayer."[7]

Therefore, in the case where there is no prayer in the Church, we will not be talking of leaders of the Church of God and there will be no flourishing leadership in the Church. For "prayer is as an intercontinental ballistic missile. With it, we can assail Satan's strongholds anywhere, even in the heavenlies."[8]

Also, leaders are killed when there is no prayer in the Church. The Scripture shows an example of a leader, James, who was arrested and executed by Herod because of lack of prayer in the Church. "About that time Herod the king laid violent hands on some who belonged to the Church. He killed James the brother of John with the sword" (Acts 12:1-2).

As soon as the Church noticed this slight error, they engaged themselves in active prayer as Peter, another leader of the Church of Jerusalem was arrested and scheduled for execution. They realised that, without them praying, they may lose another pillar of the Church: "So Peter was kept in prison, but earnest prayer for him was made to God by the Church" (Acts 12:5).

The prayer of the Church let to divine intervention, where heaven was open, and God sent an angel to deliver Apostle Peter. "Then the angel said to him, "Put on your clothes and sandals." And Peter did so. "Wrap your cloak around you and follow me," the angel told him" (Acts 12:8).

This is a great example to be followed by the Church today. The Church is called to pray for its leaders. Unfortunately, nowadays most believers don't pray for their leaders, some instead of praying for their pastors, find themselves criticising earnestly those that God established over them. Apostle Paul said to the Church in Ephesus:

Pray also for me, that whenever I speak, words may be given me so that I will fearlessly make known the mystery of the gospel, for which I am an ambassador in chains. Pray that I may declare it fearlessly, as I should.
(Ephesians 6:19-20 NIV)

The Fellowship of the First Believers

The fellowship of the first believers, again, was our model for today. The Greek word *"koinonia"* means: "fellowship", "participation", "contribution" or "sharing." The noun *"koinonia"* comes from the Greek *"koinoneo"* which means *"Act of partaking, sharing because of common interest."* It should be noted that the phrase: "Friends are one soul" was proverbial in antiquity.[9]

When Aristotle was asked, "What is a friend?" he replied, "A single soul dwelling in two bodies" (Diogenes Laertes, Lives of Eminent Philosopher 5.20). Aristotle quotes a proverb of his day, "Friends' goods are common property," and then affirms, "This is correct since community [koinonia, 'sharing'] is the essence of friendship" (Nichomachean Ethics 8.9.1 [1159b]).[10]

When we read about the life of the early Church in Jerusalem and throughout the book of Acts of the Apostles, it is obvious that fellowship, friendship, and sharing were pronounced among the members of the primitive Church. "And they devoted themselves to the apostles' teaching and the fellowship, to the breaking of bread and the prayers" (Acts 2:42). "

Another strong evidence of *koinonia* among them is that no one was considered poor among the first believers. No rule was put in place to ask believers to share their resources for distribution to all. "Rather, the early Christians respond to the necessity of others."[11]

It is written:

There was not a needy person among them, for as many as were owners of lands or houses sold them and brought the proceeds of what was sold and laid it at the apostles' feet, and it was distributed to each as any had need.
(Acts 4:34-35)

Administration & Pressure Management

The early church is our model, also in the area of administration and pressure management. In Acts 6:1-6, the bible tells us that when the workload of the Apostles increased, they did not boast saying "I can do all things through him who strengthens me" (Philippians 4:13).

Rather they looked for a way to manage the pressure on them, though it was true that they could do everything through Christ. Instead of going with fanaticism, as many believers and leaders will do today, they managed the situation with God's wisdom for Administration.

Because of their good administration, they had a successful ministry. For "Every successful organisation has good administration"[12] and so does also the Church of God. The Apostles of the Lamb (the twelve minus Judas, plus Matthias) in Acts did not rely on their capacity and mantle to manage the pressure of work, but "they appointed seven assistants (Acts 6:1-6), elected by the people and ordained them."[13]

> *One can be a spirit-filled pastor or leader with tremendous passion for God and train people, but without proper administration you cannot achieve your full results. Shepherding is ministry but the other part is administration, we see a perfect example in Genesis chapter eighteen when Moses was leading the Children of Israel. Jethro's gifts of administration helped Moses.*[14]

The Rights of the Poor, Orphans & Widows

The early congregation in Jerusalem was not only sensitive to the needs of the people when it came to the preaching of the Gospel but also cared for the poor, the orphans, and the widows. This practice was part of the Church administration and leadership and is an ongoing model for us today: "A communal sharing of earthly goods, care for the poor, especially widows and orphans characterised their fellowship."[15]

Apostle James, one of the leaders of the Church in Jerusalem said in his letter: "Religion that is pure and undefiled before God the Father is this: to visit orphans and widows in their affliction, and to keep oneself unstained from the world" (James 1:27).

This testifies that visiting and taking care of the poor, the orphans and the widows was a common practice among the first believers. It was not an option for them, but an assignment they had to do in their ministry every day.

No wonder this was part of Apostles Paul's ministry as well. Paul as the first ascension apostle learned this from the Apostles of the Lamb, establishing a parallel between the Apostles of the Lamb and the ascension apostles. In his letter to the Churches in Galatia, Apostle Paul, after presenting his work to the Apostles (Peter, James, and John) who were considered as pillars of the Church, said: "Only, they asked us to remember the poor, the very thing I was eager to do" (Galatians 2:10). His work was approved by them, but on top of that they recommended him to take care of the poor while doing the work of the ministry.

This recommendation was taken seriously by Apostle Paul, and as a good leader and servant of the Lord Jesus Christ, he passed this teaching faithfully onto his son

Timothy when he said in his first letter: "Honour widows who are truly widows" (1 Timothy 5:3). I believe, a parallel should be laid between the ascension apostles today in order to restore this godly practice that is almost forgotten in the Church today.

The Apostle in this same letter i.e. verses 3-15 gives a particular teaching on how the Church should take care of widows. It was not an option for the early Church, so should it be to the present Church. "God wants everyone of us to care for the sick, poor, strangers, orphans, widows, and anyone else who is in need. It is an act of love and mercy."[16]

Evangelism & Teaching

The early Church never functioned without evangelism and the teaching of the saints. The great commission was the centre of the mission. While reading the book of Acts of the Apostles, one can easily recognise that the disciples in the primitive Church never called themselves disciples of Christ, if they did not do what Christ Himself did: "It is enough for the disciple to be like his teacher and the servant like his master" (Matthew 10:25).

Jesus throughout His earthly ministry evangelised in the streets and villages of Israel. He was also a teacher, and He was active in the Ministry of Teaching, as we read in the Gospels. "Each day Jesus was teaching at the temple, and each evening he went out to spend the night on the hill called the Mount of Olives" (Luke 21:37 NIV).

The Lord as a good teacher with a successful ministry, taught these same principles of God's Kingdom to his disciples when He said: "Go therefore and make disciples of all nations, baptising them in the name of the Father and of the Son and of the Holy Spirit, teaching them to observe all that I have commanded you" (Matthew 28: 19-20).

Preaching the Gospel of Salvation

Today many are seeking for Church growth without preaching the Gospel of Salvation. No evangelisation, no disciples, and no discipleship, no Church growth. Also, evangelism is a sign of the presence of the Holy Spirit in the Church.

For they never rested after the Holy Spirit had come upon them. "And when they had prayed, the place in which they were gathered together was shaken, and they were all filled with the Holy Spirit and continued to speak the word of God with boldness" (Acts 4:31).

In his book "Evangelism by Fire" the writer said: "One of the ascension gifts of the Lord to His Church is that of Evangelist, but where are they?"[17] The gift of Evangelism is one of the gifts that need to be restored in the Church today. Evangelist Reinhard said again: "With the world more accessible than ever before, thousands of them (Evangelists) are busying their time away doing mundane Church jobs to which God never called them."[18]

Among the first believers, the five-fold ministries given to the Church were active, including that of an Evangelist of course. Revival can only come and be effective if the five-fold ministries are active in the Church. The ministry of the

Evangelist in Church functions like the middle finger of the hand to the body. "His ministry is more widespread than others. He reaches further. He is stifled if left in the confines of the Church."[19]

In Summary

In conclusion, the book of Acts of the Apostles remains a model and an excellent example for the present Church. This book needs to be studied with the insight of the Holy Spirit, in order to fully understand, the life of the early believers in the early Church for the proper organisation and functioning of the present Church.

The same way as Jesus learned from the Father, the Apostles of the Lamb learned from Him, and the ascension apostles from the Apostles of the Lamb. I believe that, for an excellent and successful ministry today, the present Church needs to learn from those who laid the foundation, that is the Apostles of the Lamb and the ascension apostles, with Paul being the first.

No other foundation should be laid, other than that which was laid by them; "For no one can lay a foundation other than that which is laid, which is Jesus Christ" (1 Corinthians 3:11).

The Holy Spirit is still active in the world and in the Church of God. The Acts of the Apostles are still alive, for the same Spirit who acted in them is the same, He is ready to work with us if and only we are led by Him as the early Church.

The miraculous Holy Spirit, who filled them and directed them in prayers and Church organisation is still present. He is ready to continue writing, the Acts of Apostles with the present Church of today.

For, there is no conclusion when it comes to the book of Acts of the Apostles because the present Church is called to follow the model of the first Apostles and continue writing this book throughout ages and generations in the whole world.

"But you will receive power when the Holy Spirit has come upon you, and you will be my witnesses in Jerusalem and in all Judea and Samaria, and to the end of the earth" (Acts 1:8).

Chapter 3

Only Possible By Jesus & the Holy Spirit

Revival as it was in the Early Church

As time passes, an old generation goes, and a new one comes. Throughout history, mankind has been confronted with this reality, no one can stand against this fact. Reading books about some great men of the past seems like the past has been better than the present, whatever the field. I would like to say that the present is being taught based on what was in antiquity.

Today no one can teach or learn physics, mathematics, or chemistry just to name this part of science without mentioning some substantial scientists who lived in and influenced the past centuries. Who doesn't know Albert Einstein who was influenced by Isaac Newton, who in turn was influenced by Johannes Kepler? These scientists, with other scientists of the 15th–18th centuries set a basis on what serves today as a foundation in natural science.

God-given Knowledge

By using the knowledge given to them by God, they revive the world of science, as we all know, knowledge is from God and God is the Author of science; "For the Lord gives wisdom; from his mouth come knowledge and Understanding *(science)*" (Proverbs 2:6).

Among this generation their work is still alive or better to say the work of God through them is still actual in science today. Almost everything in science turns around some of their tremendous discoveries, not to say all.

Is this to say there were more great scientists in the old days than today? No, it is far from that. Am I saying no other scientist could do what they did? No! What then? I mean to acknowledge here that reviving science today has its roots in any way in the past, for there are some laws and principles that were known unto those who were before our generation.

For sure they did not create these principles and laws by themselves, but God did it and revealed them to humans as it pleased Him; "The secret things belong to the Lord our God, but the things that are revealed belong to us and to our children forever, that we may do all the words of this law" (Deuteronomy 29:29).

King Solomon said: "What has been is what will be, and what has been done is what will be done, and there is nothing new under the sun. Is there a thing of which it is said, 'See, this is new'? It has been already in the ages before us" (Ecclesiastes 1:9-10).

In the same way as these facts are true for science and the world in general, it is also true for the spiritual realm and the Church.

Throughout ages and generations starting from the creation, through Noah, Abraham, Isaac, Jacob, Moses, the Judges, David, and the Prophets of the Old Covenant until Jesus and the first Apostles, God has always raised men to bring revival in their generation. Jesus himself while teaching had to mention some prophets who were before Him. He is from the beginning; "Jesus said to them, Truly, truly, I say to you, before Abraham was, I am" (John 8:58).

This means that, if there has ever been a revival in the history of faith and the Church, this has happened probably with Jesus Christ as the central figure. For Christ was God in the past; He is God in the present and He will be God in the future: "I am the Alpha and the Omega, says the Lord God, who is and who was and who is to come, the Almighty" (Revelation 1:8).

Elohim

This truth is very much true for the Person of the Holy Spirit as it is for Jesus. As Jesus is from the beginning, the Holy Spirit is also from the beginning. For it is written: "And the Spirit of God was hovering over the face of the waters"

(Genesis 1:2b). Talking of Jesus' the Scripture says: "In the beginning was the Word, and the Word was with God, and the Word was God" (John 1:1).

Both were with God, and both are God, referring to one God acting in plurality i.e. in Genesis 1:1 we read "In the beginning, God created the heavens and the earth." The Hebrew for God here is: *"Elohim"* which is in the plural form, but the verb *"bara"* (create) is in the singular. Meaning that both oneness and plurality are combined in this verse.

Somehow the heroes of faith of the past ages and our present age have always been rooted and inspired by the Holy Spirit, through God's Word and those who came before them.

Throughout the history of the Church, starting from Jerusalem, Judea, and Samaria with the first Apostles, passing through the great Reformation of the 16th century with Martin Luther and John Calvin, extending through William Carey and John Wesley to Charles Fox Parham, "the pioneer of Pentecost of the 20th Century,"[1] preceding the Azusa street revival with William J. Seymour, God Almighty has raised men, equipped them through the Holy Spirit and sent them to preach Jesus Christ the author of revival.

Has revival ended with them? No! God continues to anoint men and women through which revival is brought to their generation. Connecting the past generation and the present through the Holy Spirit, God gave us men like Derek Prince, David Wilkerson, Zacharias Tanee Fomum and Reinhard Bonnke who also impacted the world with the Good News of the Kingdom of God.

All these men were powerfully used by God at a certain point in the Church's history, they brought revival to this world or in their generation. We ought to note that none of them acted on their account if not through the Holy Spirit in the name of Jesus. For the power of God to have been active and manifested through them, and their generation, the Godhead was in perfect action in them i.e. without God revival wouldn't have been possible in the past generation and this is true for the present Church.

Knowing these truths, what can we say about revival through the ages until today? Is revival possible without one Person among the Godhead? Can we say there has been revival through history without God the Father, the Son, and the Holy Spirit?

What will happen to the Church if unicity in the Person of God is not preserved while serving? Can the present Church still experience a great revival as it was at the beginning of the Church on the day of Pentecost? In the following outlines, we will answer these questions in light of the Word of God.

The Beginning of Revival within the Early Church

It all started in Jerusalem, where ordinary men and women gathered in a room praying, had an encounter with the Holy Spirit.

> *And when they had entered, they went up to the upper room, where they were staying, Peter and John and James and Andrew, Philip and Thomas, Bartholomew and Matthew, James the son of Alphaeus and Simon the Zealot*

and Judas the son of James. All these with one accord were devoting themselves to prayer, together with the women and Mary the mother of Jesus, and his brothers.
(Acts 1:13-14)

As we read through verse 14, the phrase "all these with one accord were devoting themselves to prayer" cut our attention. It says, "with one accord." What is meant by this and what is the implication of this truth for those who were to have an encounter with the Holy Spirit? That is, they had a single purpose in their mind while praying, they were one as the Father and the Son are one "I and the Father are one" (John 10:30).

The reviving Spirit of God, the promised Spirit who was present during the first greatest revival mankind has ever known during the creation was coming again to bring another tremendous awakening in the streets of Jerusalem. For this to happen, unity had to be implemented among the protagonists.

In Genesis 1:2, the bible says: "The earth was without form and void, and darkness was over the face of the deep." The Holy Spirit of God through which God operated during the creation, is the same Jesus sent on the 120 disciples who were gathered in unity in the upper room devoting themselves to prayer.

Clothed with Power from on High

Before the coming of the Holy Spirit, Jesus told the first disciples: "And behold, I am sending the promise of my

Father upon you. But stay in the city until you are clothed with power from on high" (Luke 24:49).

God was preparing a revolutionary mission that would impact the whole world; very soon Jerusalem was to be impacted by empowered ordinary men and women. They had to wait until they were clothed for this mission to start. Was the promise finally sent and were they finally clothed? Yes! It is written:

> *When the day of Pentecost arrived, they were all together in one place. 2 And suddenly there came from heaven a sound like a mighty rushing wind, and it filled the entire house where they were sitting. And divided tongues as of fire appeared to them and rested[a] on each one of them. And they were all filled with the Holy Spirit and began to speak in other tongues as the Spirit gave them utterance.*
> *(Acts 2:1-4)*

Kingdom Principles & Keys that bring Revival

Unity in Prayer:

When the Pharisees were accusing Jesus of casting out demons by Beelzebub, He answered them by saying: "Every kingdom divided against itself is laid waste, and no city or house divided against itself will stand" (Matthew 12:25). Here the Lord reveals and lay a principle that cannot be ignored by any believer who wants to bring revival or be part of one.

If the actual Church wants to have a powerful success as it was seen in the past, the question of prayer and oneness needs to be solved among believers. This cannot be solved either with a denominational, a congregational, or a religious mind. For when we talk of revival in the Church, we see a transforming power acting in the person of the Holy Spirit to bring massive people to repentance and salvation, through preaching, signs, and wonders.

But could all these be possible without prayer in unity? The Scripture says:

> *And when they had prayed, the place in which they were gathered together was shaken, and they were all filled with the Holy Spirit and continued to speak the word of God with boldness. Now the full number of those who believed were of one heart and soul, and no one said that any of the things that belonged to him was his own, but they had everything in common. And with great power the apostles were giving their testimony to the resurrection of the Lord Jesus, and great grace was upon them all.*
>
> (Acts 4:31-33)

The Baptism in the Holy Spirit With Tongues as Evidence

In his book "Holy Spirit Are We Flammable or Fireproof?" the writer said:

> *The baptism in the Spirit with speaking in tongues is no new Reformation, no renovation or decoration. It is liberation and gives Christian teaching a new dimension. The baptism in the Spirit is simply typical of Who the Holy Spirit is- causing us to be "endued" with power.*[2]

One of the greatest problem the Church experiences today is the lack of power and manifestation of the gifts of the Holy Spirit. I believe that many believers still struggle when it comes to the power and the manifestation of the Spirit because many are religious believers rather than being Spirit-filled disciples. Human theories and the flesh have taken over the work of the Spirit, so instead of preaching Jesus by the Spirit or allowing the Spirit of God to reign, many will rely on their self-centred theology.

Paul the Apostle said: "And my speech and my message were not in plausible words of wisdom, but in demonstration of the Spirit and of power, so that your faith might not rest in the wisdom of men but in the power of God" (1 Corinthians 2:4-5).

Most believers instead of allowing themselves to be filled by the Holy Spirit, are still tarrying and crying to receive the Holy Spirit. Let's answer this question, is it Scriptural to tarry for the Holy Spirit? Well, the truth is that many still believe that one need to tarry or wait in order to receive the Spirit of God.

But why?! Some refer to the Scripture when Jesus said "And, behold, I send the promise of my Father upon you: but tarry ye in the city of Jerusalem, until ye be endued with power from on high" (Luke 24:49 KJV).

To Tarry or Not to Tarry?

Now let us analyse this! Jesus said, "but tarry ye in the city of Jerusalem" (Luke 24:49 KJV). Well tarrying here "is not a formula for receiving the Holy Spirit."[3] "However, if these verses were a formula for receiving the Holy Ghost, we would not have any right to take the word 'Jerusalem' out of the text."[4]

Therefore, if this is not a formula, what were the disciples waiting for? "But you will receive power when the Holy Spirit has come upon you, and you will be my witnesses in Jerusalem and in all Judea and Samaria, and to the end of the earth" (Acts 1:8).

In order words, the disciples were waiting for the day of Pentecost to come, and on this day God accomplished His promise by sending the Holy Spirit, for on that day the Holy Spirit was poured out upon the Church. This implies that, today no one ought to tarry or wait for the Holy Spirit again, for He was sent already, and He is present.

If anyone thirsts for Him, Jesus said: "Let him come to me and drink. Whoever believes in me, as the Scripture has said, 'Out of his heart will flow rivers of living water" (John 7: 37b-38).

Baptised in the Holy Spirit

Therefore, every disciple of Christ Jesus needs to be baptised in the Holy Spirit. "Without the Holy Spirit, religious faith runs on a flat battery."[5] Many Conservatives or Christians who practice a Cessationism doctrine, believe that those who speak in tongues are brainwashed believers.

Evangelist Reinhard said: "The insignia of the Spirit in this global revival is *"speaking in tongues"* (Greek *glossolalia*). It is not a new "fad" or "a cult-thing for the brainwashed."[6]

Moreover, Paul the apostle said in his first letter to the Corinthians "I thank God that I speak in tongues more than all of you" (1 Corinthians 14:8). Just by reading this portion of the Scripture reveals the importance of praying in tongues.

To have a Spirit-guided and empowered successful Christian life and ministry, every believer must be baptised in the Holy Spirit with speaking in tongues as evidence. "However, the baptism in the Holy Spirit is for all those who believe (Acts 2:38, 39); therefore, speaking in tongues as an evidence of the Spirit's infilling is also for all those who believe."[7]

The Holy Spirit who Brings Revival

Therefore, if in the New Covenant the Holy Spirit, (as the Spirit that brings revival) "is always linked with ecstatic manifestations", this implies that "when such tangible evidence was absent, it was taken as proof that people had not received the Holy Spirit."[8]

The bible teaches us that when early Christians were baptised in the Holy Spirit, some extraordinary manifestations such as tongues and prophecy followed. And this is how the early Apostles could identify if one has received the Holy Spirit or not. "And they were all filled with the Holy Spirit and began to speak in other tongues as the Spirit gave them utterance" (Acts 2:4).

> *While Peter was still saying these things, the Holy Spirit fell on all who heard the Word. And the believers from among the circumcised who had come with Peter were amazed, because the gift of the Holy Spirit was poured out*

even on the Gentiles. For they were hearing them speaking in tongues and extolling God. Then Peter declared, "Can anyone withhold water for baptising these people, who have received the Holy Spirit just as we have?"
(Acts 10:44-47)

Being Rooted in The Truth

Well, everyone has his or her one truth in the Church today. Almost every denomination, Christian network, or ministry claims to have the ultimate truth when it comes to bible theology and dogma. The truth is that; the truth is universal to one Body and not individualistic, denominational, or religious. Dr. Bill Hamon in one of his books says:

Although "structure" is good and necessary we must never lose sight of the fact that we are ONE BODY. When structure stands in the way or when we worship or idolise our structures rather than Jesus Christ who is the HEAD OF ONE BODY, then we have moved away from the Holy Spirit and Truth. (Apostles, Prophets and the Coming Moves of God [49]).[9]

So, the truth cannot be personified to a particular way of believing or practicing faith that excludes the rest of the Body of Christ. "Exclusivism leads to cults," says Dr. Bill Hamon,[10] that is why the same Author wrote further.

We must not present ourselves in a said "Association" or "Network" in such a way to imply that those who do not believe and worship the same way as ourselves are out of order with God or are in some kind of error. This is not the prerogative of some kind of Pope Initiative, whether it is the Catholic, Charismatic, Pentecostal, Evangelical, Kingdom, Faith, Prophetic or the Apostolic kind (Apostles, Prophets, and the Coming Moves of God 49).[11]

Having discussed on what does not stand for the truth, what or who is then the Truth? The answer is Jesus. For, He said: "I am the way, and the truth, and the life. No one comes to the Father except through me" (John 14:6). This explains why revival will never happen, unless the Ultimate Truth of God, who brings revival is in action.

Christ Preached

For Jesus is the Word of God; "In the beginning was the Word, and the Word was with God, and the Word was God" (John 1:1). Revival starts when bible truth on the person of Jesus is being restored and preached. Apostle Paul said: "For I decided to know nothing among you except Jesus Christ and him crucified" (1 Corinthians 2:2).

So, only Christ crucified, is worthy to be preached and no other god or divinity should preach except Jesus. Through Him and by Him comes revival. Even the Holy Spirit of God came to glorify the Father through the message of the cross, that is why Jesus said of Him: "He will glorify me, for he will take what is mine and declare it to you" (John 16:14). The first Christians did not only know this truth, but they practiced this.

I believe that a much greater revival is coming, but until then the Church as a whole needs to come back to bible truth. Yes, for it to come, the Church needs to come back to the original Gospel of the Kingdom of God, which was preached by the first Apostles. Philip the Evangelist, after being ordained as a Deacon by the Apostles, understood this principle and grabbed the key to revival.

One of the greatest revivals which is recorded in the bible, after that which happened on the day of Pentecost, was that of Samaria. What led to this revival? The book of Acts of the Apostles in chapter 8 reveals to us the message that was preached to the people in Samaria. This message was not based on humane theory, theology, or doctrine, but it was a simple message full of the power of God, for Philip preached Christ the essence of the Gospel.

> *Philip went down to the city of Samaria and proclaimed to them the Christ. And the crowds with one accord paid attention to what was being said by Philip, when they heard him and saw the signs that he did. For unclean spirits, crying out with a loud voice, came out of many who had them, and many who were paralysed or lame were healed. So, there was much joy in that city.*
> (Acts 8:5-8)

Furthermore, when talking about the Truth, we cannot ignore this bible truth on the Person of the Holy Spirit. As it was already mentioned, the oneness of God is unique and vital for revival. Jesus the Lord talking of the Spirit said, "But when the Helper comes, whom I will send to you from the Father, the Spirit of truth, who proceeds from the Father, he will bear witness about me" (John 15:26).

That is, the Holy Spirit is the Spirit of Truth and not of manipulation or emotions. He comes with the truth; He is the Truth. So, for revival to come in the Church, the Holy Spirit should be one inspiring the Gospel we are to preach.

Nowadays many have departed from the truth to embrace a diluted, manipulated, and emotional full messages. Many have forgotten that standing out of the truth brings grieve and not revival. Revival comes only through Spirit-filled believers and not through religious believers. After the day of Pentecost, there was another revival outbreak in Jerusalem (See Acts 4:8-32).

The Spirit of Truth Rested upon Them

The Apostles were filled with the Holy Spirit whenever they had to preach, in order words they were filled with the Truth, for the Spirit of Truth rested on them, in them, and was with them. "Then Peter, filled with the Holy Spirit, said to them, "Rulers of the people and elders" (Acts 4:8), "and they were all filled with the Holy Spirit and continued to speak the Word of God with boldness" (Acts 4:31b).

Therefore, massive salvation, signs, and wonder can only show up if and only if disciples of Christ stand on the message of the Truth, preach the Truth by the power of the Holy Spirit, and love the Truth. For the devil is out there to deceive those who do not hold up unto the truth.

"The coming of the lawless one is by the activity of Satan with all power and false signs and wonders, and with all wicked deception for those who are perishing, because they refused to love the truth and so be saved" (2 Thessalonians 2:9-10).

Since we mentioned manifestations, signs, and wonders as being the product of revival or the result of a Spirit-filled message based on the Truth, does this mean that every manifestation is from the Spirit of God? No! But why?

Derek Prince in his book, "Protection from Deception" said, "It is very essential to understand that signs and wonders do not determine truth! Truth is already determined and established, and it is the Word of God."[12] "Sanctify them in the truth; your Word is truth" (John 17:17).

The Dangers of Deception

Finally, what could we say? Should one run after manifestation or after the truth? Well, I believe that Christians should seek first the ultimate revealed truth of God, which is His Word in order not to be deceived. For one of the greatest dangers in these end times is deception.

He who flees from deception by harkening to the revealed Truth of God in His Word is wiser than he who says, "It could never happen to me", the truth is that "it has already happened to that person, because that person is saying something could never happen that Jesus said would Happen."[13]

Jesus said: "Watch out that no one deceives you... and many false prophets will appear and deceive many people... For false messiahs and false prophets will appear and perform great signs and wonders to deceive, if possible, even the elect" (Matthew 24:4, 11, 24 NIV).

In Summary

It can be concluded that, as time advances, the old generation goes and a new arises. Generations and methods may differ from one another, but spiritual principles, keys and laws never change, that is: spiritual principles based on the foundation of the truth, which is the Word of God, has not change, for Jesus said: "Heaven and earth will pass away, but my words will not pass away" (Matthew 24:35).

Preaching Jesus Christ alone and His Word through the power of the Holy Spirit is the essence and the catalyst of revival. All believers need to be filled with the Holy Spirit with evidence of speaking in tongues, for revival only comes through men and women who have accepted Jesus as Lord and Saviour and who have been baptised with the Holy Spirit.

Revival started with the Holy Spirit; therefore no one can claim or attempt to bring revival if he or she has not been impacted by the Holy Spirit.

Christians of this age must follow the biblical example of devotional prayers in unity, and with one soul in order to experience revival in its fullness with great signs and wonders as a result and a confirmation of the True Gospel of Christ proclaimed.

It is written: "And they went out and preached everywhere, while the Lord worked with them and confirmed the message by accompanying signs" (Mark 16:20). "While God also bore witness by signs and wonders and various miracles and by gifts of the Holy Spirit distributed according to his will" (Hebrews 2:4).

God is always ready to bring a new move of the Spirit, He is ready for the next move, for the Holy Spirit was already given and He is present in the Church, ready to use every humbled, loved, and Spirit-filled believer.

If the Truth, Jesus is preached based on the revealed Truth of God, God will work in this generation as He did in early Church, for "Jesus Christ is the same yesterday and today and forever" (Hebrews 13:8).

CHAPTER 4

The Kingdom of God has Come

Extra Biblical Doctrines

Over the centuries, the Church of God has passed through many reformations. The Gospel of the Kingdom of God has been preached and sometimes twisted. Many extra biblical doctrines have been introduced in the Church. The true and original message of the Kingdom of Heaven has been changed, and became for some a religion, for others a cultural paradigm, while for others a business, and became for some a place and weapon to best practice spiritualism, magic, and divination all in the name of Christ.

Scanning through the evolution of the history of the Church while looking at all the biblical practices in comparison with extra biblical doctrines, can we say that the Kingdom of God has come to all? Or is it fair to say the Kingdom of God has come to some and others not? What then! At the beginning of His ministry, the Lord Jesus said: "The time is fulfilled and the Kingdom of God is at hand; repent and believe in the Gospel" (Mark 1:15).

Heresies & Malpractices

Thus, is it because some heresies and malpractices have entered the Church, that every supernatural manifestation will be quoted as fake instead of being a proof of the manifestation of the Kingdom of God? No! far from that, but, the truth is that there is no Kingdom of God without the manifestation of the Power of God. Jesus said to the Pharisees attributing God's power to the devil: "But if it is by the Spirit of God that I cast out demons, then the Kingdom of God has come upon you" (Matthew 12:28).

Following the example of Jesus Christ and the first Apostles, can the Good News of the Kingdom of God be preached without what makes it essence? Apostle Paul said: "For the Kingdom of God does not consist in talk but in power" (1 Corinthians 4:20).

Are we saying we ought to run after power and manifestation? No! he who does that is closer to seduction or is already seduced. "For false christs and false prophets will arise and perform great signs and wonders, so as to lead astray, if possible, even the elect. See, I have told you beforehand" (Matthew 24:24-25). What are we then saying? "The Christian should aim at pursuing fruit bearing rather than struggling for power. It is the Holy Spirit who empowers us for ministry."[1]

Therefore, knowing that it's the Holy Spirit who empowers and gives us the grace to bear fruit, the practice of healing the sick, casting out demons, and raising the dead in the Church will be discussed in this work as the fruits of the manifestation of the Kingdom of God by the power of the Holy Spirit.

For the Holy Spirit is the manifested power of God in the Kingdom of God. "and my speech and my message were not in plausible words of wisdom, but in demonstration of the Spirit and of power, so that your faith might not rest in the wisdom of men but in the power of God" (1 Corinthians 2: 4-5).

The Principles of The Kingdom of God

What is the Kingdom of God?

The word Kingdom originates from the ancient Greek word *"basileia"* meaning a royal palace. Basileia comes from the Greek word *"basileus"* meaning emperor, or king (king someone who exercises royal authority and sovereignty). Literally, *"basileia"* means Kingdom or royal power.

Dominion or Reign:

Addressing the Kingdom as dominion or reign simply means exercising kingly power. It is written: "and he will reign over the house of Jacob forever, and of His Kingdom, there will be no end" (Luke 1:33). God through His angel Gabriel is speaking of the everlasting King in God's Kingdom, Jesus. He was to reign on the house of Jacob forever.

This confirms the prophecy of Daniel the prophet when he said: "And in the days of those kings the God of heaven will set up a Kingdom that shall never be destroyed, nor shall the Kingdom be left to another people. It shall break in pieces all these kingdoms and bring them to an end, and it shall stand forever" (Daniel 2:44).

As it is written, "Your Kingdom come, Your will be done, on earth as it is in heaven" (Matthew 6:10), God sent His son Jesus Christ the King of kings to come and exercise His kingly power here on earth as it is in heaven in order to destroy and demolish the active working force of darkness in the world.

When This force is in direct opposition to the Kingdom of God. This force is the kingdom of darkness and is led by Satan, who is actively opposing and affecting the world systems: culture, media, government, economy, education, family, religion, politics, education, philosophy, entertainment, and the arts.[2]

In other words, "If we are going to win the battle, we must know the enemy. We must not allow ourselves to remain in ignorance, but must acquaint ourselves with what the scriptures teach."[3] So being aware of this reality will give the believer an insight on how to exercise God's power here on earth and in the Church rather than being fake or being crushed by the devil. "so that we would not be outwitted by Satan; for we are not ignorant of his designs" (2 Corinthians 2:11).

Dominion's Realm

This can be defined as a group of people living in a territory under a kingly rule. The word, dominions, here shows the hierarchy under which these people are submitted. That is a set of people ruled by a higher and supreme authority who has a superior power over them.

Example: the United Kingdom is ruled by a king who has authority over his citizens as their king and his authority cannot be extended over other citizens belonging to other kingdoms unless he conquers them. That is the king of England has no authority over Cameroonians for instance, unless he conquers Cameroon and makes it part of his kingdom.

The bible teaches us that the first kingdom established by man was that of Babel, Erech, Accad, and Calneh in the Land of Shinar. This was a rebellious Kingdom, for it was against the Word of God (Genesis 9). Nimrod was the founder of these kingdoms: "Cush fathered Nimrod; he was the first on earth to be a mighty man. He was a mighty hunter before the Lord. Therefore, it is said, "Like Nimrod a mighty hunter before the Lord." The beginning of his kingdom was Babel, Erech, Accad, and Calneh, in the land of Shinar" (Genesis 10:8-10).

The Kingdom of God (He Basileia Tou Theou)

The phrase "Kingdom of God" comes from the Greek *"he basileia tou Theo"* meaning the royal palace of God or the royal power of God. Who speaks of a royal palace or power surely speaks of the king ruling this palace with royal authority or power. Therefore, Jesus is the ruling King in the Kingdom of God.

Generally, in a Kingdom, no one knows what is better for the people living in that kingdom than the King. This is why Jesus, as the King of kings among all existing kingdoms has prepared His Church to enter God's Kingdom. Jesus came to reveal and teach the secrets of the Kingdom to the elected ones, that is why He said: "But seek first the Kingdom of God and his righteousness, and all these things will be added to you" (Matthew 6:33).

The Kingdom of God came with Jesus Christ

Preaching and the baptism of repentance: The bible reveals that John the Baptist started his ministry with the preaching of the Gospel saying, "Repent for the Kingdom of heaven (GOD) is at hand" (Matthew 3:2). As announced by Isaiah the prophet, John the Baptist was the voice who cried in the wilderness to prepare the way for the coming King and His Kingdom: "A voice cries: "In the wilderness prepare the way of the Lord; make straight in the desert a highway for our God" (Isaiah 40:3).

This prophecy was repeated by Matthew in His Gospel when he said, "For this is he who was spoken of by the prophet Isaiah when he said, The voice of one crying in the wilderness: Prepare the way of the Lord; make His paths straight" (Matthew 3:3). This confirms the fulfilment of this Scripture with the coming of John.

John the Baptist did not only preach the Gospel of the Kingdom to prepare the heart of the people but he also Baptist in water those who repented for the forgiveness of their sins. By so doing he was making a way for the Lord to come, that's why he said: "I baptise you with water for repentance, but He who is coming after me is mightier than I, whose sandals I am not worthy to carry. He will baptise you with the Holy Spirit and Fire" (Matthew 3:11, see also Mark 1:1-8).

The Preaching of Jesus

In his book "Healing and Deliverance A Present Reality" Dr. Alan says:

> *This then was the purpose and destiny for which Jesus had been predestined. The salvation of man. Jesus had not come to perform signs and wonders – these were just His calling card – proof that the Kingdom of God had come. For the miracles that Jesus performed such as the casting out of demons, healing the sick and power over nature, were the indication and proof that Satan's power on this earth had been broken.*[4]

The Lord Jesus started His ministry by preaching the Gospel of the Kingdom saying: "The time is fulfilled and the Kingdom of God is at hand; repent and believe in the Gospel" (Mark 1:15). Do we need to border ourselves to wait for the Kingdom of God again? No, for it is already among us and it started with Jesus. This message of the Kingdom was announced by the prophets in the Old Testament.

For Jesus came not only to set up His Kingdom but also to proclaim liberty to the captives and recovery of sight to the blind "The Spirit of the Lord is upon Me because He has anointed Me to proclaim Good News to the poor. He has sent

Me to proclaim liberty to the captives and recovering of sight to the blind, to set at liberty those who are oppressed" (Luke 4:18).

The Greek word used for proclaim here is "kerusso" meaning to herald (as a public crier) especially when it comes to divine truth (the Gospel), i.e. to announce publicly. Therefore, Jesus also came to announce publicly the Gospel of the Kingdom of God: "And He went throughout all Galilee, teaching in their synagogues and proclaiming the Gospel of the Kingdom and healing every disease and every affliction among the people" (Matthew 4:23).

The Manifestation of God's Power through Healing, Deliverance & Raising the Dead

Dr. Alan wrote: "Jesus' miracles also have another purpose, to show us what the Kingdom of God is like and to reveal a glimpse of God's love, peace and joy to those that He has predestined to be adopted as His sons."[5]

Throughout the Gospels, we read that Jesus always healed the sick, cast out demons, raised the dead, cleansed the lepers, and opened the eyes of the blind while preaching the Gospel of the Kingdom. When the Pharisees came to the Lord and asked when the Kingdom of God would come, Jesus answered them saying: "The Kingdom of God is not coming with signs to be observed or with a visible display; nor will people say, 'Look! Here it is!' or, 'There it is!' For the Kingdom of God is among you [because of My presence]" (Luke 17:20-21 AMP).

The Lord emphasises here that the Kingdom of God is not a one-man show, nor a spectacular scene like in a Hollywood movie, but he declares that because of His presence, God's Kingdom has come among us. Since this Kingdom is among us, the royal power of God can henceforth be exercised on this earth through the manifestation of the Holy Spirit: "But if it is by the Spirit of God that I cast out demons, then the Kingdom of God has come upon you" (Matthew 12:28).

The Kingdom of God is at Hand

The Lord commands His disciples to do the same as they go on preaching the Gospel "And proclaim as you go, saying, 'The Kingdom of heaven is at hand.' Heal the sick, raise the dead, cleanse lepers, cast out demons. You received without paying; give without pay" (Matthew 10:7-8). Interesting what the Lord says here, freely you have received and freely you shall give.

Unfortunately, today many will preach the Gospel, heal the sick, or even cast out demons and ask for a ransom after this. Here we no longer talk of the message of the Kingdom of God. For the Good News of the Kingdom is freely given to us by God through the Holy Spirit.

At the cross of Calvary, Jesus paid the price for the deliverance of all those who come to him by faith; the only thing God wants from us here is our faith "Our freedom from Satan's power, however, only becomes effective in our lives when we individually come to Jesus Christ by faith, confessing our sins and turning from our own way, and yielding to Him as Lord."[6]

Jesus never saw the sick and needy who came as an opportunity to reap them off as we see in some Churches today, where the Good News of the Kingdom has become a business and a way to become rich. Sadly, Jesus did not die on the cross for that, but for the Salvation of all those who come to Him freely with faith "For whatever reason they came, Jesus saw them through the eyes of a shepherd who had compassion for His sheep."[7]

In Summary

To summarise, the Kingdom of God is among us. As Jesus said to John the Baptist who was asking him if He was the one to come, He said: "Go and tell John what you have seen and heard: the blind receive their sight, the lame walk, lepers are cleansed, and the deaf hear, the dead are raised up, the poor have Good News preached to them" (Luke 7:22); He is saying the same thing to us today especially to anyone who doubt that His Kingdom is already present among us.

The kingdom of darkness has been destroyed already, all and everyone is called to come to Jesus by faith to receive healing, deliverance, and salvation. For with the presence of the Kingdom of God, there is healing for the sick, deliverance for the demonised, and resurrection for the dead; "Jesus healed all who came to Him, whether they had diseases, severe pain, demon-possessed, those having seizures, even the paralysed were not disappointed."[8]

Being aware of this reality should not in any way lead us astray in search of spiritism or fake manifestation all in the name of Jesus, rather we should stay spiritually awake like those in the early Church. "It is interesting to see that people were more spiritually aware of those with demonic problems than we are today, in our sophisticated Western world."[9]

Because they were awakened and sought first the Kingdom of God and its righteousness, early Christians never went to mediums or spiritualist meetings for their spiritual comfort. "But seek first the kingdom of God and his righteousness, and all these things will be added to you" (Matthew 6:33).

CHAPTER 5

The Prayer of Faith

In Christ Alone

When we talk of prayer, one may first, think of religion. Throughout the history of mankind, men have been praying and addressing their prayers to some divinity. We see prayer being practiced by different religions. Every one of these religions claims to pray to the true God.

For example, in Buddhism, they pray to Buddha, Muslims will pray to Allah; while Christians will pray to God the Father through Jesus Christ: "Truly, truly, I say to you, whatever you ask of the Father in my name, he will give it to you" (John 16:23b).

One thing to be appreciated here is that not every prayer

is meant to be called the prayer of faith. For all do not pray to the one true God, who has set a way in Jesus Christ through which every man can come to Him; "Jesus said to him, "I am the way, and the truth, and the life. No one comes to the Father except through me" (John 14:6).

Except through Jesus, there is no real prayer or no prayer of faith, instead, there is spiritism, which is "one of the innocent faces of the occult."[1] Usually, those who pray to other divinities or other gods, don't pray the prayer of faith we are about to discuss in this work.

Avoid False Religious Practices

Every religion, faith confession, or denomination practicing spiritism is a false religion or a cult. That is: "A false religion is any which denies or ignores Jesus Christ as the only Lord and Saviour of the world and the only One who can forgive sins and give us eternal life."[2]

Some of these religions where people pray, or as stated earlier, practice prayer through spiritism or spiritual incantation but deny Jesus Christ as Lord and Saviour are: "Jehovah's Witnesses, Mormonism, Moonies, Christian Science, Scientology, Rajneesh, Yoga and Yoga exercises (part of Hindu worship), Reincarnation, Eastern Meditation, Hinduism, Islam, Buddhism."[3]

Are we saying prayer or the prayer of faith is only best practiced among Christians? No! not as such, for in this generation many fake prophets and teachers have entered the Church and corrupted the true prayer with their false teachings full of heresies. Instead of praying to God through Jesus Christ, today many are seen praying to their "small gods, or idols" all in the name of "men of God."

Others will pray to saints and others to angels forgetting that; it is prohibited by the Word of God to pray to the creature; "And when I heard and saw them, I fell down to worship at the feet of the angel who showed them to me, but he said to me, "You must not do that! I am a fellow servant with you and your brothers the prophets, and with those who keep the words of this book. Worship God" (Revelation 22:9-10).

True Prayer vs Yoga or Spiritual Incantations

Sadly, the Christian prayer which is supposed to set a base and serve as an example when it comes to the prayer of faith, has turned to something else nowadays. Some prayers in the Church today are not different from spiritual incantations. Other Christians will even practice yoga in the Church of God and call it a new style of prayer and worship, while others will make hypocritical noise in the name of shouting and say they are praying.

"And when you pray, you must not be like the hypocrites. For they love to stand and pray in the synagogues and at the street corners, that they may be seen by others" (Matthew 6:5).

Let me reaffirm that this is in no way a criticism of how people pray in the Church but it is a call to examine the spirit that is sometimes behind certain extravagant manifestations and spiritual activities. For it is written "Beloved, do not believe every spirit, but test the spirits to see whether they are from God, for many false prophets have gone out into the world" (1 John 4:1).

Knowing that the days are bad and that the spirit of deception has entered the Church, every genuine child of God must have a discerning spirit in order not to fall into the trap of the devil when it comes to prayer, for through prayer we can connect to the true and only God or to another divinity which is not God.

The Nature of Prayer

What is prayer? Prayer can be defined as asking and receiving by faith; "And whatever you ask in prayer, you will receive, if you have faith" (Matthew 21:22). The Greek word for prayer in the New Testament is *"euche"* which means *"a wish"* expressed as a petition to God or a *"vow."* The verb form here is *"euchomai"* meaning *"to wish"* or by implication *"to pray to God."*

Dr. Alan in his book *'Prayer, Touching the Heart of God'* says; "Prayer before anything else is relationship" and "the true essence of all praying is Touching the Heart of God."[4] This means prayer is also a spiritual communication between humans and God.

Addressing prayer as a spiritual weapon, Derek Prince in his book *'Spiritual Warfare'* says: "Prayer is an intercontinental ballistic missile."[5] What is a ballistic missile? "This is a missile that is launched from one continent and directed by an advanced guidance system to a target in a completely different continent to destroy an assigned target."[6] Therefore "Prayer is a weapon in the hand of the believer."[7]

Praying by Faith

The bible says without faith it is impossible to please God "And without faith it is impossible to please him, for whoever would draw near to God must believe that he exists and that he rewards those who seek him" (Hebrews 11:6).

This implies that every prayer done without faith or out of faith can't please God and hence he who prays as such, cannot receive from God. Rather he who prays the prayer of faith should be ready to receive an answer from God: "This prayer (command) should always be based on God's will, which is revealed in His Word. It never contains an – if."[8]

It is not universal to speak of the *'Prayer of Faith'* without mentioning James 5:15 which says: "And the prayer of faith will save the one who is sick, and the Lord will raise him up. And if he has committed sins, he will be forgiven." Thus, prayer as an exercise of faith is the key to seeking God's will in regard to healing.

What is Faith?

Faith can simply be seen as Trust plus Obedience to God. It is defined in the Word of God as "the assurance of things hoped for, the conviction of things not seen" (Hebrews 11:1), and thus "So faith comes from hearing, and hearing through the Word of Christ" (Romans 10:17).

Talking of faith that proceeds from the Word of God, Dr. Alan wrote: "The Word of faith is in our hearts. The mouth speaks it out. It does not depend on our spirituality or on how many years we have been Christians (Smith Wigglesworth would simply say, 'Only believe...')."[9] For, "Our faith must depend on God and not in our ability or circumstances, but in God alone."[10]

The Power of the Tongue & the Word

Many in the Church still ignored the power that is in the tongue or in the Word of God. As a result of this ignorance, many Christians wouldn't use their mouth properly to say or proclaim the right word at the right time. Dr. Alan wrote: "The tongue is very powerful and we need to guard it. In the prayer of faith the tongue is important. We release our faith by our tongue."[11]

I will even say it takes time, wisdom, and revelation to come to the knowledge of this biblical truth. Spiritual carelessness and lack of spiritual awareness when it comes to the revealed truth of God on how to use our tongue can cost one his or her life. This is simply because "Our tongue will have more effect in the spirit realm when we learn how to control and guard it. Jesus' tongue was always guarded."[12]

Let's analyse what the bible says in Proverbs 18:21; "Death and life are in the power of the tongue, and those who love it will eat its fruits." It says, "Those who love it will eat its fruits." Love what? the adequate or the inappropriate use of the tongue. Because there is power in the tongue, one should guard and use the tongue properly.

In the above-mentioned verse, the word 'death' comes first and then 'life' second. What does this mean? It simply implies what comes out first of our mouths if we don't use it as we ought to, is death.

Thus, it is vital and mandatory for every believer to be wise and apply wisdom and discernment whenever one is talking. How can this wisdom be applied then? The bible gives us a simple answer to that; "Keep your heart with all vigilance, for from it flow the springs of life" (Proverbs 4:23).

Therefore, if one wants to enjoy the fruits of the power of the tongue leading to life, one needs to guard his or her heart in the Lord: "The good person out of the good treasure of his heart produces good, and the evil person out of his evil treasure produces evil, for out of the abundance of the heart his mouth speaks" (Luke 6:45).

Overall, he who wants to pray efficiently and get the results (the fruits of life), should first learn how to use his or her tongue, for it is written: "But no human being can tame the tongue. It is a restless evil, full of deadly poison. With it we bless our Lord and Father, and with it we curse people who are made in the likeness of God" (James 3:8-9).

Praying by Faith According to God's Will

Jesus prayed by faith while seeking the will of God. If we want to get the same result as Jesus our Lord, we are called to pray the same way as the master did. Before the cross of Calvary, the Lord Jesus prayed to the Father saying: " And going a little farther he fell on His face and prayed, saying, "My Father, if it be possible, let this cup pass from me; nevertheless, not as I will, but as you will" (Matthew 26:39).

Every disciple of Christ is called to pray according to the will of God. Then praying according to His will opens the heavens and pours back on us the many blessings that come from God as a result of an answered prayer. "And this is the confidence that we have toward Him, that if we ask anything according to His will He hears us. And if we know that He hears us in whatever we ask, we know that we have the requests that we have asked of Him" (1 John 5:14-15).

God will only answer a prayer when this is done according to His will. Out of the will of God, one should not expect to have an answer. Because God is just, He will only give us what He judges as good for us: "If you then, who are evil, know how to give good gifts to your children, how much more will your Father who is in heaven give good things to those who ask Him!" (Matthew 7:11), and where His will and sovereignty are preserved and exalted.

Having Assurance in Prayer

He who has assurance has the faith to receive from God and he who lacks assurance is deprived of faith which is the key to receiving from God. E.M. Bounds said: "God giving His Son is the assurance and guarantee that He will freely give all things to him who believes and prays."[13]

Having the assurance that God has answered our request banns the way of doubt during prayer. Hence praying without doubt is like buying a house without cash. Unbelievable to man, but true to God, for "All things are possible for one who believes" (Mark 9:23).

In Summary

In Conclusion, every child of God should bear in mind that the prayer of faith is far better than just talking anyhow. Then prayer is not spiritism or any kind of spiritual jargon done in order to receive something, but it is an active communication with God the Almighty through Jesus Christ. He who prays according to the will of God and as His Word recommends will receive a positive answer from God who answers prayers: "O you who hear prayer, to you shall all flesh come" (Psalm 65:2).

Because the prayer of faith does not come from the misusing of the tongue, every disciple of Christ is called to guard his or her tongue, for through the tongue one can build or destroy. Faith is the result of hearing God's Word and he who hears and puts into practice the Word of God can exercise faith during prayer and enjoy its fruits as God answers the prayer done by faith. "And whatever you ask in prayer, you will receive, if you have faith" (Matthew 21:22).

Chapter 6

Christ in Science (Laminin Protein)

The Molecular Signature of Christ in Science

Throughout ages, millennia, centuries, and decades the world has been evolving with science and religion being its backbone. A parallel can be drawn between science and religion with each claiming to have the ultimate truth of the origin of life. Many scientists and religious authorities over time have come to the conclusion that science and religion can't intersect together.

It seems like there is no angle of interconnection between both, no perpendicular line of either one or the other can be drawn to overlook the matter closely. The existence of God has always been questionable to the known mind of the *Homo sapiens* under the sun.

I will say that the philosophy of life hasn't been that easy to understand since the Dark Ages and it's still not an easy go for the human brain. Many generations have come and passed, and it seems like the questions about God and science have gradually evolved from elementary interrogatories to puzzles of unsolved mysteries.

It seems like as time passes it becomes easier for science to prove biological theories against religion or monotheistic beliefs of humans than showing the other way round, that human beings are always limited when it comes to solving the questions of the natural visible, and the divine invisible world.

Many will try to explain God's existence or abstractness from a logical view. Okay! that's fine, for man is a syllogistic reasoner and his brain loves what is rational. Thus, irrationality always elicits questioning and hence leads to scepticism; "a philosophy that was popular for several hundred years in Ancient Greece and later in Rome."[1]

Keeping an Open Mind

One of its main teachings was: "You shouldn't rely on what you believe to be true. You might be mistaken. Everything can be questioned, everything doubted. The best option, then, is to keep an open mind."[2]

Is it really true that everything can be questionable? Well from a purely natural and humanistic perspective, that can be true, but what about the immaterial world? I will say questionable to a certain point; for how can the finite question the infinite?

A popular biblical prophet named Job once questioned God and He answered him by saying: "Who is this that darkens counsel by words without knowledge? Dress for action like a man; I will question you, and you make it known to me. Where were you when I laid the foundation of the earth? Tell me, if you have understanding" (Job 38:2-4).

Should we Adopt the Ancient Skeptical Philosophy of Pyrrhonism?

Therefore, if none of us was there from the beginning of life, does it make sense to adopt Pyrrhonism to judge what is true or what isn't when it comes to the subject of a God creator of everything? Or to what extent does being sceptical help humans know the truth about the origin of life?

I believe that scepticism has influenced not only people living in the era around 270 BC but also many in our modern-day world; although it's human to a certain degree to be sceptical when it comes to implausible facts. Instead, moderate scepticism will suggest that "one should get closer to the truth, or at least to reveal how little we know or can know."[3]

Thus, "there is a great tradition of moderate scepticism, of questioning assumptions and looking closely at the evidence for what we believe, without attempting to live as if everything was in doubt all of the time."[4]

How can one get closer to the truth then? Or is it logical to the human brain that there is a hidden truth about the origin of life, and Jesus as the Lord and Saviour of all? For it is written: "And you will know the truth, and the truth will set you free" (John 8:32).

Well, here we will answer these questions not only from a biblical perspective but also by using biology; the science of life and living organisms, molecular biological methods and modern technologies with the aid of which human life can be understood better and unsolved problems can be solved. After all, I am not saying, that biology or technology is the ultimate solution, but I mean here that it is part of the solution so far as there is a tangible explanation of what has been discovered.

The Secret things belong to the Lord

Lest is it better to say as Solomon the king, "Is there a thing of which it is said, See, this is new? It has been already in the ages before us" (Ecclesiastes 1:10). Of course there is nothing new under the sun, for one can only discover what exists or existed already, though it may be hidden.

As a believer and a scientist, I would like to thank God the first scientist, who said in His Word "The secret things belong to the Lord our God, but the things that are revealed belong to us and to our children forever, that we may do all the words of this law" (Deuteronomy 29:29). What I mean here is that, thanks to God who made science evolved and through it many discoveries unveiling the hidden secrets of the ages.

Christ in Science (Laminin Protein)

One of the many discoveries is the Laminin protein. Since its discovery, Laminin has not only been viewed as a molecule in molecular biology for scientists but also as a revelation to the body of Christ and the rest of the world for some believing scientists. In this outline, we will try to understand Laminin protein from a biological angle as well as from a spiritual view in order to answer the main question of this chapter.

Can science and Christian belief match? What is so special about this protein, is that we should focus our attention on it to try to understand the origin of life and the Christian faith and science.

God will Open our Eyes

I believe that God will open our eyes and understanding to apprehend the structure and the function of this protein as a step ahead to set up a base for faith in the unbelieving world of science. He will open the door for unbelieving scientists to find rational explanations, with both a scientific and a spiritual language, and to come to the knowledge of God through Christ whose cross is mirrored in the cross-like protein Laminin.

This outline is not only for scientists or unbelievers but also for Christians, for it will help every Christian to have a balance in his or her faith when it comes to being both a scientist and a Christian without any compromise. I say this because many believing Christians have lost their faith because of science and many believing scientists have lost their science because of their faith.

Does it make sense to lose faith in favour of science or vice versa? I will say No! For, God is not the author of confusion. He is not against science, because knowledge belongs to Him: "The fear of the Lord is the beginning of knowledge; fools despise wisdom and instruction" (Proverbs 1:7). The same as science is from God, faith is also from God through Jesus the perfecter of our faith (Hebrews 12:2).

What is Laminin Protein?

The Role of Laminin in the Body mimics the Role of Jesus in the World: Proteins are very essential for life and the human body has more than a hundred thousand variety of proteins that play many different roles in the body. Laminin is one of those proteins, and it is part of the extracellular matrix in humans and animals.

Laminin was discovered by Rupert Timpl in 1979 during biochemical analysis of the matrix-like material secreted by the Engelbreth-Holm-Swarm (EHS) mouse sarcoma.[5]

The extracellular matrix (ECM) is a complex of proteins and other molecules that provide support and attachment for cells inside organs. "Laminin has *"arms"* that associate with other Laminin molecules to form sheets and bind to cells. Laminin and other ECM proteins essentially *"glue"* the cells (such as those lining the stomach and intestines) to a foundation of connective tissue."[6]

The Structure of Laminin, Hazard or Revelation?

Among the thousands of proteins found in the human body, Laminin appears with a special structure. I mean there are a lot of proteins and molecules in the body with special and beautiful structures; after all, did God not say everything He created was very good: "And God saw everything that He had made, and behold, it was very good. And there was evening and there was morning, the sixth day" (Genesis 1:31).

If everything created by God is very good, why do we then specify that Laminin is a special one? Well, I believe that every genuine Christian who encounters the structure of Laminin will say that. Why, simply because it has a cross-like shape. Indeed, we can't just rely on its structure and say it is special. Thus, we need to look at other characteristics of the protein to comprehend why from a Christian and scientific background we can conclude that it is a special protein.

Let us now try and answer the question about Laminin being the fruit of hazard or being a revelation. Well, scientists, atheists, and philosophers may see it from an evolutionary perspective. Around 460-430 B.C, the Sicilian philosopher Empedocles, a proto-evolutionist *(people who developed some kind of theory of evolution before Charles Darwin and Alfred Russel Wallace)* believed that "the elements come together randomly and sometimes form parts of animals and plants—a head here and a leg there—and that in turn these sometimes combine to make functioning organisms."[7]

Charles Darwin in his published article on *Origin of Species*, argued "that organisms are the products of a process of gradual natural change—evolution—fuelled mainly by a mechanism that he called *"natural selection."*[8]

If scientists, unbelievers, and philosophers could visualise Laminin from an evolutionary or a Darwinism perspective, how should a Christian approach the molecular structure of Laminin then? It is better not to fall into a religious trap and start saying that the protein itself is Jesus because of its cross-like structure, that will sound heretical instead of Christian theology.

Moreover, the cross was only a natural wood on which the Lord Jesus was crucified; but is it because it was only a tree that it has no meaning to the Christian faith? No! For spiritually, the cross is more than just being a piece of wood; "For the Word of the cross is folly to those who are perishing, but to us who are being saved it is the power of God" (1 Corinthians 1:18).

Beyond the Sceptical Thinking of the Human Brain

HalleluYaH, the cross is the power of God to save all those who believe or will believe in the finished work of Jesus Christ on the cross of Calvary. Analysing everything in detail while observing the structure of Laminin, we can conclude that, the cross-like structure of this protein shouldn't just be seen as a natural thing, but this should go far beyond the sceptical thinking of the human brain.

In the same way as the cross on which the Lord Jesus was crucified, was just a piece of wood; Laminin is just a protein found in the human body with its structure being a cross, though it shouldn't be neglected or ignored. I believe that this cross-like structure is more than just a simple molecule or the result of a Big Bang theory, which aims mostly to explain the origin of the universe without God as the main character.

This structure reveals more than what we can say and observe from a biological view. It is not just a protein but is the glue of all our cells and tissues in the human body i.e. holding them all together, mimicking the role of Jesus in the universe; for it is written: "And He is before all things, and in Him, all things hold together" (Colossians 1:17).

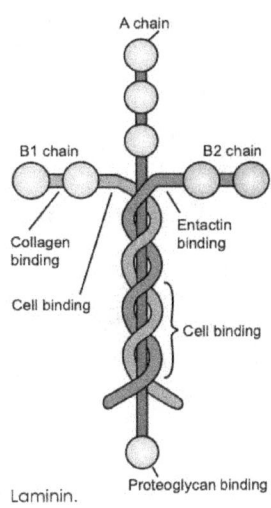

Pastor Louie Giglio, once suggested that:

> *The cross-shaped protein is scientific evidence that Christ is holding our bodies together. His theological proposition suggests that Colossians 1:17 is directly referencing the cross-shaped Laminin protein for two reasons:*
>
> *(1) It is shaped like the cross that Jesus was crucified upon, and*
>
> *(2) Laminin's primary function of binding our cells together is the meaning of the latter part of verse 17, "in Him all things hold together."*[9]

It should be noted that Laminin protein cannot be equated to Jesus and His finished work on the cross, but I believe that its cross-like structure shouldn't be ignored, for the bible says: nature itself teaches us (1 Corinthians 11:14).

Though there can be a lot of discussion around Laminin from both sides (Christians and scientists) to try and proof or disproof Colossians 1:17 as being connected to Laminin or not. I will say, that both Christian scientists and unbelieving scientists should see the beauty of God the creator of everything through this protein.

With or without Laminin God will remain Almighty, for He made Laminin and not the reverse. Is the creation itself not revealing the hands of a God behind everything that exists? If it does, why should we not then appreciate the beauty and the might of God the creator through Laminin?

"All things were made through Him, and without Him was not anything made that was made" (John 1:3). "For by Him all things were created, in heaven and on earth, visible and invisible, whether thrones or dominions or rulers or authorities—all things were created through Him and for Him" (Colossians 1:16).

Therefore, everything including Laminin was made by Him for a purpose, and I believe that God can reveal Himself to many unbelieving scientists through this tiny protein, for its structure is not the fruit of hazard, for with God there is no hazard, rather there is truth and evidence. HalleluYaH, God's Word can only be and remains the ultimate truth through which both believers and scientists can hold on, to come to the knowledge of the true and one God who is in Christ Jesus the Lord.

In Summary

To conclude, if we remove God from science, science will not exist or have a meaning, and if we practice faith without

God, we are just being religious. Knowledge comes from God but while seeking knowledge, both Christians and scientists need to be balanced and humble enough to recognise the place and the role of God in everything that exists, for "the God who made the world and everything in it, being Lord of heaven and earth, does not live in temples made by man" (Acts 17:24).

Christians should not run away from science and scientists should not run away from faith. Instead of adopting a sceptical mind when it comes to the question of faith and science, I believe that both protagonists should allow God to come into play, to understand the mysteries of the creation and the creatures. For the human brain, technics and science is limited but God is not limited. He knows every detail of our universe and the things present in the world.

Christians doing science should even be aware not to fall into the trap of evolution theory. Instead, I believe that; Christians should pray to God, who is above science and who knows and reveals everything to reveal Himself to scientists through the science they practice.

For who talk of science also say there may be discoveries; but who allows humans to discover if not God Himself, for "the secret things belong to the Lord our God, but the things that are revealed belong to us and to our children forever, that we may do all the words of this law" (Deuteronomy 29:29).

If Apostle Paul in Athens could confront some Epicurean and Stoic philosophers (Acts 17:18) with both the Gospel and their own philosophy, "In Him we live and move and have our being; as even some of your own poets have said, "For we are indeed his offspring (Acts 17:28), why can't we today confront scientists, atheists and agnostics with the Gospel and Laminin?

Endnotes

Chapter 1 The Primitive Church

1. Apeabu, John A. A History of the Early Church (05 BC-AD 451). Zaria, Nigeria: Faith Printers International, 2020. p2.

2. Ibid., p1.

3. Asare, Benjamin Ayim. Discover Your Ministry in the Local Church. Novara, Italy: BENCOM Publications, 2016. p15.

4. Apeabu, John A. A History of the Early Church (05 BC-AD 451). Zaria, Nigeria: Faith Printers International, 2020. p5.

5. Bonnke, Reinhard. Holy Spirit Revelation & Revolution: Exploring Holy Spirit Dimensions. E-R Productions LLC, 2007. p15.

6. Ibid., p17

7. Maldonado, Guillermo. Divine Encounter with the Holy Spirit. New Kensington, USA. Whitaker House, 2017. p9.

8. Bonnke, Reinhard. Holy Spirit Revelation & Revolution. p15.

9. Asare, Benjamin Ayim. Discover Your Ministry in the Local Church. p12.

10. Ibid., p18.

11. Ibid., p18.

12. Pateman, Alan. His Faith, Positions Us for Possession. Lucca, Italy: APMI Publications, 2014 (updated version 2020). p42.

Chapter 2 As Described by the Book of Acts

1. Burge, Gary M., Cohick, Lynn H., and Green, Gene L. The New Testament in Antiquity. Michigan, USA: ZONDERVAN, 2009. p230.

2. Pateman, Alan. Apostles: Can the Church Survive without Them? Lucca, Italy: APMI Publications, 2012. p33.

3. Ibid., pp35-36.

4. Burge, Gary M., Cohick, Lynn H., and Green, Gene L. The New Testament in Antiquity. p231.

5. Ibid., p234.

6. Prince, Derek. Spiritual Warfare. New Kensington, USA: Whitaker House, 1987. pp103-104.

7. Asare, Benjamin Ayim. Discover Your Ministry in the Local Church. Novara, Italy: BENCOM Publications, 2016. p113.

8. Prince, Derek. Spiritual Warfare. p104.

9. Burge, Gary M., Cohick, Lynn H., and Green, Gene L. The New Testament in Antiquity. p235.

10. Ibid., p235.

11. Ibid., p235.

12. Asare, Benjamin Ayim. Discover Your Ministry in the Local Church. p115.

13. Pateman, Alan. The Age of Apostolic Apostleship. Florence, Italy: Published by APMI Publications. Copyright ©2017 (updated version 2020). p191.

14. Asare, Benjamin Ayim. Discover Your Ministry in the Local Church. p155.

15. Apeabu, John A. A History of the Early Church (05 BC-AD 451). Zaria, Nigeria: Faith Printers International, 2020. p75.

Endnotes

16. Asare, Benjamin Ayim. Discover Your Ministry in the Local Church. p124.

17. Bonnke, Reinhard. Evangelism by Fire: Keys for Effectively Reaching Others with the Gospel. Charisma House, 2011. p6.

18. Ibid., p6.

19. Pateman, Alan. Apostles: Can the Church Survive without Them? p53.

Chapter 3 Only Possible by Jesus & the Holy Spirit

1. Pateman, Alan. The Early Years, Anointed Generals Past and Present (Part One of Four). Florence, Italy: Published by APMI Publications. Copyright ©2012 Alan Pateman. p18.

2. Bonnke, Reinhard. Holy Spirit: Are we Flammable or Fireproof? Orlando, USA. Publisher: Christ For All Nations (CFAN) Publication Date: November 14, 2017. p126.

3. Hagin, Kenneth E. The Holy Spirit and His Gifts. USA: Faith Library Publications, 1974 (2nd ed. edition January 1, 1991). p75.

4. Ibid., p75.

5. Bonnke, Reinhard. Holy Spirit Revelation & Revolution: Exploring Holy Spirit Dimensions. Orlando, USA: E-R Productions LLC, 2007. p100.

6. Ibid., p100.

7. Hagin, Kenneth E. The Holy Spirit and His Gifts. p90.

8. Bonnke, Reinhard. Holy Spirit Revelation & Revolution. p100.

9. Pateman, Alan. The Age of Apostolic Apostleship. Florence, Italy: Published by APMI Publications. Copyright ©2017 (updated version 2020). p25.

10. Ibid., p26.

11. Ibid., p26.

12. Prince, Derek. Course Syllabus: THE-304 Protection from Deception. Florence, Italy: Published by APMI Publications. Copyright ©2022 Alan Pateman Ministries. p4.

13. Ibid., p3.

Chapter 4 The Kingdom of God has Come

1. Asare, Benjamin Ayim. The Pursuit of Power Versus Fruits. Novara, Italy: BENCOM Publications, 2019. p. vii.

2. Pateman, Alan. Healing and Deliverance, A Present Reality. Lucca, Italy: Published by APMI Publications. Copyright ©1994 (updated versions 2018, 2020). p13.

3. Ibid., p14.

4. Ibid., p85.

5. Ibid., p85.

6. Ibid., p27.

7. Ibid., p80.

8. Ibid., p89.

9. Ibid., p89.

Chapter 5 The Prayer of Faith

1. Pateman, Alan. Healing and Deliverance, A Present Reality. Lucca, Italy: Published by APMI Publications. Copyright ©1994 (updated versions 2018, 2020). p139.

2. Ibid., p139.

3. Ibid., p139.

4. Pateman, Alan. Prayer, Touching the Heart of God (Part Two). Lucca, Italy: Published by APMI Publications. Copyright ©2012. p12.

5. Prince, Derek. Spiritual Warfare. New Kensington, USA: Whitaker House, 1987 USA. p104.

6. Ibid., p104.

7. Asare, Benjamin Ayim. Discover Your Ministry in the Local Church. Novara, Italy: BENCOM Publications, 2016. p113.

Endnotes

8. Pateman, Alan. Prayer, Touching the Heart of God (Part Two). p26.

9. Ibid., p26.

10. Ibid., p25.

11. Ibid., p27.

12. Ibid., p27.

13. Ibid., p133.

Chapter 6 Christ in Science (Laminin Protein)

1. Warburton, Nigel. A Little History of Philosophy. Padstow, UK: Yale University Press Publications. Copyright © 2011, Nigel Warburton. p15.

2. Ibid., p15.

3. Ibid., p20.

4. Ibid., p20.

5. Timpl, Rupert, et al. Laminin—a Glycoprotein from Basement Membranes. Journal of Biological Chemistry, vol. 254, no. 19, 10 Oct. 1979, pp. 9933–9937. PMID: 114518. https://doi.org/10.1016/S0021-9258(19)83607-4.

6. Purdom, Georgia. Laminin and the Cross Is There a Connection. Published in Answers in Depth, Vol. 3, 2008, pp83-84; https://assets.answersingenesis.org/doc/articles/aid/v3/laminin-cross.pdf.

7. Ruse, Michael. Darwinism as Religion: What Literature Tells Us About Evolution. New York, USA: © Oxford University Press 2016. p1.

    See also: Bowler, Peter J. Evolution, the History of an Idea. California, USA: © University of California Press 1984.

8. Ibid., p.xv.

9. New Life Exchange, Laminin: Evidence of God's Existence? 6 Dec. 2017, newlifeexchange.com/2017/12/06/laminin-evidence-gods-existence/.

Note: the picture on page 95 has been taken from https://assets.answersingenesis.org/doc/articles/aid/v3/laminin-cross.pdf.

Other information on this subject:

Matlin, K.S., et al. Article Title: Laminins in Epithelial Cell Polarization: Old Questions in Search of New Answers. Journal Title: Cold Spring Harbor Perspectives in Biology. Volume and Issue Number: vol. 9, no. 10. Publication Date: 3 Oct. 2017. Article Number: article a027920. DOI: https://doi.org/10.1101/cshperspect.a027920

Bible translations

- Unless otherwise indicated in this chapter, all scriptural quotations are taken from The Hebrew-Greek Key Word Study Bible: English Standard Version (ESV). Edited by Spiros Zodhiates, series ed. Warren Patrick Baker, AMG Publishers, 2013.

- Scripture references marked AMP are taken from the Amplified® Bible (AMP), Copyright © 2015 by The Lockman Foundation. Used by permission. All rights reserved." La Habra, CA 90631. USA.

- Scriptural quotations marked KJV are taken from the King James Version of the Bible Copyright © 1982 by Thomas Nelson, Inc. USA.

- Scripture references marked NIV are taken from the HOLY Bible, NEW INTERNATIONAL VERSION®, NIV® Copyright ©1973, 1978, 1984, 2011 by Biblica, Inc.® Used by permission. All rights reserved worldwide.

❖

Ministry Profile

Martial LeBras NONO, a servant of GOD and an apostle of JESUS CHRIST by the will of GOD the Father and the HOLY SPIRIT. Apostle NONO is an ordained minister, and he is the founder and leader of *Go and Preach to All Nations Ministry, and Grow With Christ,* by the grace of GOD: *"For so the Lord has commanded us, saying, I have made you a light for the Gentiles, that you may bring salvation to the ends of the earth"*(Acts 13:47).

He was born in Cameroon and later traveled to Germany to further his studies, where he obtained a Bachelor of Engineering in Biotechnology, at the University of Applied Sciences Jena. He also holds a Bachelor of Arts in Christian Theology from LifeStyle International Christian University. He is currently pursuing his studies in medicine.

NONO is a committed disciple of CHRIST who started serving GOD at the age of 15 as a Sunday School Teacher at the Evangelical Church of Cameroon. He is very passionate and committed to the work of the Kingdom of GOD, especially for souls winning and he's very active in Evangelism and disciples making around the Nations. He has preached and taught the Gospel of CHRIST in many countries around the globe, such as in Africa, Europe, and Asia. With his team, he organizes crusades, retreats, and outreach programs. NONO also has a unique and Spirit-filled ability to minister to the poor, the prisoners, the orphans, and the widows, as the LORD also sent him to this specific population, to bring them the love of CHRIST in a living way.

To Contact the Author

Please email:

Martial LeBras Nono
Email: nono.martial@yahoo.fr or
contact@growwith-christ.com

*Please include your prayer requests
and comments when you write.*

PUBLISH YOUR BOOK WITH

APMI Publications
a division of Alan Pateman World Missions

APMI Publishing and Publications is committed to providing you with an affordable and easy way to publish your books making them available as paperback, hardcover, and/or eBook copies on international outlets.
Contact us today!

Dr Alan Pateman
Senior Editor/Publisher

www.alanpatemanworldmissions.com/publications
Tel. 0039 366 329 1315; publications@alanpatemanworldmissions.com

www.ingramcontent.com/pod-product-compliance
Lightning Source LLC
Chambersburg PA
CBHW061952070426
42450CB00007BA/1319